# GET INTO THE
# BIBLE

## FROM FIRST CREATION TO NEW CREATION:
THE UNFOLDING PLAN OF GOD IN SCRIPTURE

### by John Richardson

THE
GoodBook
COMPANY

Get Into the Bible
John P. Richardson
Published by The Good Book Company
Copyright © John Richardson, 1994
All Rights Reserved

The Good Book Company
Elm House, 37 Elm Road,
New Malden, Surrey KT3 3HB
Tel: 0845-225-0880
Fax: 0845-225-0990
email: admin@thegoodbook.co.uk
web: www.thegoodbook.co.uk
MPA Books (Australia): 9 Cudgee Close, Baulkham Hills, NSW
2153,

Scripture taken from the HOLY BIBLE, NEW INTERNATIONAL,
VERSION COPYRIGHT © 1973,1978,1984 by International
Bible Society. Used by Permission of Hodder and Stoughton
Limited.

ISBN UK: 1 873166 08 7
Cover Design: Jon BRadley
Printed in Hong Kong

# About this Booklet

I have tried to make this book as readable as possible. Therefore the style and layout may seem a little strange in places. I have used BLOCK CAPITALS and **bold** lettering to make it easier to identify parts of the text of which you should take particular note. You are not supposed to SHOUT when you read them. I have also used *italics* throughout for certain key words like promise or fulfilment. These identify themes which run through the whole Bible. Occasionally I have inserted boxes where there are issues I wanted to discuss which are not essential to the main flow of the argument. I suggest you read these anyway!

PART ONE of this booklet is a general overview of the Bible. PART TWO is concerned with methods of Bible study.

Books I have found helpful and would recommend for further study include:

• *Gospel and Kingdom*, Graeme Goldsworthy (Paternoster Press). The original inspiration for this booklet came from here. Read it!

• *Postcard from Palestine*, Andrew Reid (St. Matthias Press). An excellent 'work book' with many useful exercises.

• *Unlock the Bible*, Stephen Motyer (Scripture Union). Introduces the different types of literature in the Bible and their significance.

• *How to Read the Bible for All it's Worth*, G. Fee and D. Stuart (Scripture Union). A bigger version of Motyer's book, looks at some harder issues.

• *The New Testament Documents: Are they Reliable?*,
F. F. Bruce (IVP). A perennial reprint well worth the money.

• *Lion Let Loose*, John Sergeant (Paternoster Press). A good
introduction to the concept of themes and plot in the
Gospels.

• *According to Luke*, David Gooding (IVP). Especially good for
the chapter on 'Aims, methods and explanations'.

• *The Faith of Israel*, W. J. Dumbrell (Apollos/IVP). Takes you
through every book of the Old Testament. Read it with your
Bible open.

# Contents

# INTRODUCTION

This booklet is written for people who:

- **are Christians**
- **value reading the Bible**
- **have been reading it for maybe one or two years**
- **have perhaps been using 'study notes'**
- **BUT—feel there must be more to the Bible than they are now getting out of it.**

It will not tell you everything there is to know about Bible study—that is a lifetime's work. Nor does it set out to prove the truth of the Bible, or to answer all the questions you might have. **Its aim is to help you study the Bible more effectively for yourself.** In the process, it will introduce you to some of the ideas and insights which are available to the experts (who are really just 'experienced beginners') but which are often contained in large and expensive books. This booklet is not a substitute for those other books—indeed it freely uses ideas taken out of them. (I have given the titles of some of these on pages 3 and 4.) My hope is that you will go on and read some of them for yourself, especially if you find this booklet too 'condensed'. But my immediate aim is to save you time, trouble and expense, and to point you in the right direction for more fruitful Bible study.

I am assuming three things from the beginning:

**1. That the Bible is God's written Word.**
**2. That the basic message of the Bible is clear to any Christian reader. (The older generations of Christians referred to this as the 'perspicuity' of Scripture—**

meaning you could see through it clearly, like
'Perspex'!)
3. That the more we know about the Bible and how to
study it, the more effective our study will be.

# An overview of the Bible

# What is the Bible?

I am assuming you have already read at least some of the Bible. You will have realised from this that the Bible—a word which just means 'the Book'—is a collection of smaller books (sixty-six in all) in a variety of styles and on a variety of subjects.

The Bible translations we have today are mostly based on the Hebrew 'Masoretic Text' for the Old Testament and the best Greek texts now available for the New Testament. New Bible versions are NOT just updates of older versions. Producing a new Bible translation is not like playing 'Chinese Whispers' ! A lot of work goes into researching and understanding the best texts available, which is why new translations sometimes differ from the old.

The **order** of books in our **Old Testament** follows that of a very early (3rd century BC) translation made by Jewish scholars of the Hebrew Bible into Greek. This was called the Septuagint, from the Latin for seventy, since it was supposed to have had seventy translators. You will often see it referred to as the 'LXX'. The layout of the Hebrew Bible and the LXX may be compared as follows:

| HEBREW | LXX |
|---|---|
| **Law** | |
| Five 'Books of Moses'. | Five 'Books of Moses'. |
| **Prophets** | |
| "Former" (Joshua, Judges, 1 & 2 Kings, 1 & 2 Samuel). "Latter" (3 'Major', i.e. Longer and 12 'Minor', i.e. shorter, prophets). | Mixture of history and 'wisdom' books from Joshua to Song of Solomon. 'Major' prophets & Lamentations. |
| **Writings** | |
| Everything else. | Daniel & 12 'Minor' prophets. |

As you can see, the structure of the Hebrew Bible is more theologically systematic than that of the LXX, and you can perhaps now understand why Jesus referred to the Scriptures as "the Law and the Prophets".

Our division of the Bible into two parts—the Old and New Testaments—is not altogether helpful. You will often find a blank page between the two sections of the Bible. As one English scholar has said, the best thing you can do with this page is to tear it out! **The Bible is ONE book telling ONE story**.

# How does the Bible work?

This may seem a peculiar question, but it conveys what I am trying to get across in this booklet. The Bible, through the presence of the Holy Spirit in the believer, is a LIVING WORD which, when properly used, works to change us! But if it is to do this most effectively then, like a car, a painting or a computer, we must understand something about its design and purpose.

**The Bible is the book of *salvation*. It tells us about *salvation* and brings us into *salvation*.**

The name "Jesus" (which is the Greek version of "Joshua") actually means "Saviour". We could say that the purpose of the Bible is to tell us ABOUT Jesus and to bring us TO Jesus. The Old Testament points forward to Jesus, the New Testament points backwards to Jesus, but both have Him at the centre:

**Old Testament ➡ Jesus ⬅ New Testament**

We can see this in Jesus' own words: "This is what I told you while I was still with you; Everything must be fulfilled that is written about me in the Law of Moses, the Prophets and the Psalms." (Luke 24:44).

But for a lot of people this is a puzzle. How CAN we say that the Old and New Testaments are both about Jesus'? Some people find it hard to believe they talk about the same GOD, let alone the same Saviour! I must admit this used to puzzle me, too. I used to look on the Old Testament as something like "God's Plan that Failed", or even worse, "God's Plan that Was Never Intended to Succeed in the First Place"! I can now see this was nonsense. How could **God** have a plan that didn't work—especially one that took two thousand years for Him to realise this? To understand the Bible properly we must understand that it is about ONE plan that SUCCEEDED. And to do this, we must look at the Big Picture first—the way in which the whole Bible describes God's *salvation* plan. This involves bringing together **four elements**.

### 1. HUMAN HISTORY AND THE EXPERIENCE OF *SALVATION*

The quickest way to get an idea of how the Bible works is to look at the **human experience of *salvation* in history**. We can draw this out like a graph. In the period before Jesus was born it looks rather like a ski-jump:

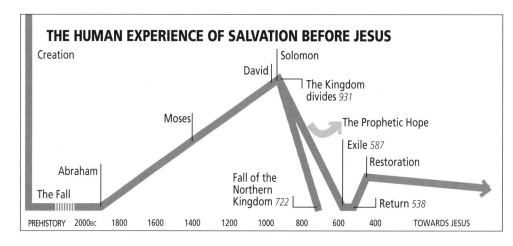

In the beginning, the human race was created by God **in His image, to rule the world** and to do so in fellowship with Him and with one another. This 'image-bearing rule' is our TRUE NATURE and is part of the end-goal of God's plan. Yet, though it may sound peculiar to say so, the first great event in *salvation-history* was the Fall—the initial rebellion of the human race against God! It is because of the Fall that we need *salvation*. However, in the 'pre-historic' time between the Fall and the choosing of Abraham, there was little progress in the experience of *salvation* by the human race. What we see in this period (covered by Genesis 1-11) is repeated examples of God acting both to *judge* and to *save* the human race.

With God's choice of Abraham, however, (Genesis 12, about 2,000 BC) we begin to see some progress. **For the next 2,000 years, from Abraham to Jesus, the human experience of *salvation* is linked almost exclusively to the physical history of Israel.**

From Abraham to David (2,000-1,000 BC, up to 1 & 2 Samuel), this history is largely one of blessing. The archetypal '*salvation* experience' in this period is the EXODUS, where the people are brought out of Egypt **not** into the 'Promised Land' but to Mount Sinai, where they receive **tokens** of God's blessing—the Tabernacle, the Commandments and the Sabbath.

**It is of particular significance that Israel receives only the tokens of God's blessing at Sinai**. This implies that there is a **greater *fulfilment*** still to come (since they are only tokens) and that this blessing is not tied to the Promised Land (since the tokens are given outside the Land). We can see this idea of a greater *fulfillment* developed later in the letter to the Hebrews. The **tabernacle** signifies God's dwelling with mankind as in Eden, yet God does not yet truly dwell on the earth (l Kings 8:27, cf. Revelation 21:3). The **commandments** signify God's rule through deciding 'good and evil' as in Eden, yet the law is not yet written on the human heart (Ezekiel 36:26-27 cf. 2 Corinthians 3:7-8). The **Sabbath** signifies God's rest—the ultimate state of blessing—as in Eden, but rest is not experienced in this world (Psalm 95:11, cf. Hebrews 4:3).

The period after the entry into the Promised Land (Joshua, Judges) saw many times of affliction, but with the establishment of the *Kingdom* the general tendency of the '*salvation*' graph is upwards. The high point of Israel's national history as an experience of *salvation* is the reign of *King* Solomon. Yet it is also the 'watershed', since from the end of Solomon's reign onwards (931 to 586 BC, covered by 1 & 2 Kings, paralleled in 1 & 2 Chronicles) the 'graph' runs downwards. The depths are plumbed when the nation is finally conquered and many of the people are taken into EXILE in Babylon (587/6 BC—see Jeremiah, Lamentations, Ezekiel and Daniel).

This is followed by the RESTORATION (538 BC—see Ezra and Nehemiah, Haggai, Malachi and Zechariah), and for a while things seem to be improving again. Yet these *hopes* are not *fulfilled*, and until the coming of Jesus the nation experiences a succession of further conquests, though some measure of political stability is achieved under the Romans.

## 2. THE PROMISE OF GOD AND THE KINGS WHO FAILED

The second element we must bring into the picture is the ***promise of God*** (which is included in the concept of 'Covenant'—another word for 'Testament').

**The first expression of this *promise* is in Genesis 3:15, in God's words to the serpent who had tempted Eve into falling**: "I will put enmity between you and the woman, and between your offspring and hers; he will strike your head, and you will strike his heel." We should take special note of the singular "he" and "his" because the question then becomes: "To whom does this refer?" One of the main reasons behind the recording of genealogies (ancestral name-lists) in Genesis 1-11 is the search for this descendant. Cain and Abel prove to be 'dead ends'—the one more literally than the other—but the descendants of Seth carry the *promise* on into the future.

**Though there are other aspects to it in Genesis 1-11, the next stage of the *promise* we will consider is its renewal to Abram**. His name meant 'Exalted Father', but he was unable to have children! God's *promise* to him is, "I will make you into a great nation, and I will bless you; I will make your name great, and you will be a blessing. I will bless those who bless you, and whoever curses you I will curse; and all peoples on earth will be blessed through you." (Gen.12:2-3, repeated and reinforced at intervals later). We should especially note three elements of this promise:

1. **Personal blessing: "I will bless you; I will make your name great".**
2. **National blessing: "I will make you into a great nation".**
3. **World blessing: "you will be a blessing. I will bless those who bless you, and whoever curses you I will curse; and all peoples on earth will be blessed through you".**

The attention now focuses on the one who becomes Abra**ha**m (meaning 'Father of Many') and his descendants through Isaac (Gen.17:15-21) and Jacob.

**The *promise* is re-established in Exodus 2:24**: "God heard (the Israelites) groaning, and he remembered his covenant with Abraham, with Isaac, and with ... Jacob." To 'remember' means here 'to act on'. God chooses this point to act on his *promise* to the Patriarchs and the result is the commissioning of Moses and the deliverance from Egypt.

The covenant with the descendants of the Patriarchs is confirmed in blood at Sinai (Exodus 24:8). However, the focus of attention narrows in the succeeding years from the nation to the *King,* for with David there is a further development. David's personal ambition is to build a house (i.e. the Temple) for God. **However, God turns the tables by *promising* to build a 'house' (i.e. a Dynasty) for David**: "Now I will make your name great, like the names of the greatest men of the earth. And I will provide a place for my people Israel and will plant them so that they can have a home of their own and no longer be disturbed [...] The LORD declares to you that the LORD himself will establish a house for you. When your days are over and you rest with your fathers, I will raise up your offspring to succeed you, who will come from your own body, and I will establish his *kingdom*. HE IS THE ONE who will build a house for my Name, and I will establish the throne of his *kingdom* for ever. I will be his father and he shall be my son." (2 Samuel 7:9b-14)

We can see the 'seed' motif from Eden repeated here in what is said about David's offspring. Notice also how elements of the *promise* to Abraham reappear. God now *promises* to make David's name great and he again promises blessing for his people. However, we are still looking forward since even David is not the final recipient of the *promise.*

In the reign of Solomon the high point of national blessing is reached and for a time it seems that the promised world-blessing will follow (cf. the visit of the Queen of Sheba, I Kings 10:1-13). But things go disastrously wrong.

Because of his worship of other gods, the *Kingdom* is taken away from Solomon: "Since ... you have not kept my covenant and my decrees ... I will most certainly tear the *kingdom* away from you" (l Kings 11:11). **Yet even at this stage, God does**

**not go back on his *promise* and instead extends it to Solomon's son**. He continues, "Yet I will not tear the whole *kingdom* from him, but will give him one tribe for the sake of David my servant." (l Kings 11:13)

Thus the promise remains. But as successive *Kings* lead the nation further and further into sin, the nation experiences God's *judgement* and the *Kingdom* goes into a decline from which it never fully recovers. Even today, whilst the Jews are still a people and Israel is again a nation, they are NOT A *KINGDOM*. What, then, has been happened to the *promise?*

### 3. THE FUTURE *KINGDOM* AND THE PRESENT TENSION

As the experience of *salvation* in the history of Israel first reaches a peak and then declines, a new element of **Prophetic *Hope*** comes in. Its main feature is **an ideal future in tension with a disappointing present**. This *hope* is present already in the Psalms (e.g. Psalm 85). It is even more evident in the "Latter" prophets (those who primarily wrote their prophecies rather than delivering them orally). A number of themes emerge in these prophecies, including a new Exodus, a restored *Kingdom* and an era of peace and justice. However, other elements suggest a **radical renewal of Creation**: "The wolf will live with the lamb, the leopard will lie down with the goat ... the cow will feed with the bear ... and the lion will eat straw like the ox" (Isaiah 11:6). In fact, a **New Eden** is in view: "The LORD will surely comfort Zion ... he will make her deserts like Eden" (Is.51:3). Other themes include:

- the Day of the LORD (or, "that Day")
- *Judgement*
- *Salvation* of the Gentiles ("the nations"—see below)
- the Rule of God through his Anointed *King*:

**"Rejoice greatly, O Daughter of Zion! Shout, Daughter of Jerusalem! See, your king comes to you, righteous and having *salvation* ... He will proclaim peace to the nations. His rule will extend from sea to sea and from the River to the ends of the earth."**
*(Zechariah 9:9,10)*

Isaiah declares that this requires a "new heavens and a new earth" (65:17). The old creation order is simply not up to it! Through Jeremiah, however, it is also declared that we are talking about a **New Covenant Relationship** (i.e. a 'New Testament'—'Testament' and 'Covenant' being the same word) with God since the old human race is not up to it either:

> **"'This is the covenant that I will make with the house of Israel after that time,' declares the LORD. 'I will put my law in their minds and write it on their hearts.'"** *(Jeremiah 31:33)*

The original *promise* has now become a '*super-promise*'—a *prophetic hope* which seems to be increasingly 'out of this world'. However, far from being *fulfilled* at the Restoration after the Exile, it is simply pushed further forward.

> **The Prophetic *hope* becomes further and further removed from, and in tension with, the present historical experience. It is essentially 'other-worldly'. Its *fulfilment* increasingly rests not on an 'improvement in' but a 'TRANSFORMATION OF' the human condition.**

Taken on its own, the Old Testament is thus a book with a direction and a *hope*, but no conclusion. But the Old Testament should not be taken on its own!

### 4. THE *PROMISE FULFILLED*

Matthew's Gospel begins, "A record of the genealogy of Jesus Christ the son of David, the son of Abraham: Abraham was the father of Isaac, Isaac the father of Jacob ..." (Matthew 1:1 and so on for 17 verses.) It seems a strange way to begin the Gospel—the greatest piece of 'good news' in the world! But can you now see why Matthew does this? We are being told what has happened to the *promise*. Matthew spells it out for us (compare this with our 'Ski-Jump' outline): "Thus there were fourteen generations in all *from Abraham to David*, fourteen *from David to the exile to Babylon*, and fourteen *from the exile to the Christ*." (1:17) This is Matthew's view of history, leading to the *fulfilment* of the *promise*.

Time and again the New Testament books declare to us that **"no matter how many *promises* God has made, they are 'Yes' in Christ"** (2 Corinthians 1:20). In Christ the human experience of *salvation* reaches its climax: "The blind receive sight, the lame walk, those who have leprosy are cured, the deaf hear, the dead are raised" (Matthew 11:5). In Christ the dwelling of God is on earth (John 1:14). In Christ we see the human race as it should be: able to rule the world, control the weather, walk on water and multiply bread and wine. In Christ we see a man able to live a life of perfect obedience to God. Most importantly, in Christ we see a man able to crush Satan under his feet. The New Testament tells us that Jesus is what the Old Testament was about: "You diligently study the Scriptures because you think that by them you possess eternal life. These are the Scriptures that testify about me," (John 5:39), "What God *promised* our fathers he has *fulfilled* for us, their children, by raising up Jesus." (Acts 13:32).

**The GOSPEL is that Jesus is the one in whom the promise of God finds its fulfilment:**
**"Paul ... called to be an apostle and set apart for the gospel of God—the gospel he *promised* beforehand through his prophets in the Holy Scriptures regarding his Son, who as to his human nature was a descendant of David ... Jesus Christ our Lord."**
*(Romans 1:1-4)*

With the coming of Christ, however, there is a significant change in the focus of God's work for Jesus is finally rejected by Israel. From here on, *salvation* is experienced not in the socio-political *Kingdom* of Israel but in the multi-national ***Kingdom* of God**. The world-blessing *promised* through Abraham has now begun in earnest!

Even in the New Testament, however, there remains a tension between present experience and future *hope*. In Jesus we see things as they **will be** but in ourselves we see things as they **still are**. This tension will only finally be resolved at Christ's return when he will establish the *Kingdom* of God on earth. The Epistles of the New Testament largely deal with the problems of this remaining tension, while the Book of Revelation points towards, and allows us a glimpse of, the final establishment of the *Kingdom*.

# Putting it all together

Having seen these four elements, **1. Human History and the Experience of *Salvation*, 2. The *Promise* of God and the Kings who Failed, 3. The Future *Kingdom* and the Present Tension** and **4. The *Promise Fulfilled***, what are we to make of them? There are a number of ways in which they will help us in our study of the Bible:

> **FIRST**, we will see that the Bible is not a series of red-herrings and dead-ends out of which God pulls some kind of resolution, but ONE BOOK telling ONE STORY—of the plan and purpose of God to *save* mankind.
>
> **SECOND**, we will understand each book of the Bible IN ITS OWN CONTEXT OF *SALVATION-HISTORY*. At some stage you should go back to the 'ski-jump' diagram and see how each book fits into its period.
>
> **THIRD**, we will interpret each part of the Bible by remembering that the *promises* of God are only fully and finally revealed in Jesus. The experience of *salvation* will be related to the book's position in relation to the coming of Jesus.
>
> **FOURTH**, we will see that even for Christians there is a present tension between the *hope* and the *fulfilment* of the *promise*.

### TWO 'WORKED EXAMPLES'

To show what this means, we will look at two 'worked examples'. The first concerns **Noah**. In what way are we to understand and learn from his story? He is often (like almost every good character in the Old Testament) presented basically as an example of 'faith'—and Hebrews 11:7 shows that, at one level, this is right. But can we say more, or is the Old Testament just a compendium of 'faithful saints' for us to imitate?

Noah's personal context is 'pre-historical', but he appears in the middle of a series of cataclysmic acts of *judgement* and *salvation* from the expulsion from Eden to the scattering at Babel. In his day he is seen as the 'Great *hope*': his name sounds like 'Comfort' and it is hoped that, "He will comfort us in the labour and painful toil of our hands caused by the ground the LORD has cursed." (Genesis

5:29, compare with 2:17). The question for his generation is therefore "Will Noah *fulfil* the *promise* of *salvation?*"

In one sense Noah performs even better than expected. As the world goes from bad to worse and comes under God's *judgement* (6:5-7), so Noah "found favour in the eyes of the LORD" (6:8). Noah does indeed become the instrument of *salvation,* and the *promise* is renewed to him (9:1-17). But we soon see that he is not able to overcome sin and Satan, nor is he able to communicate his own righteousness to the new world! All too soon we read of his getting drunk and of his son Ham's sexual mockery of him (9:20-23).

Ultimately, Noah teaches us more about God's faithfulness than his own faith. He tells us more about human sinfulness than the victories we can achieve through faith. Above all, he shows us our need of a greater Saviour from an even greater *judgement* to come. Reading the Bible in the light of the lessons above allows us to see more in Noah than an example of faith and to detect in his story elements important to the preaching of the Gospel.

The second example, from a different era, is that of **Amos**. He is often held up as the preacher of social renewal: "let justice roll on like a river, righteousness like a never-failing stream!" (5:24) In his writings he speaks of the coming "day of the LORD" (5:8) which will be a day of *judgement* on Israel (9:1-10). However, he also talks of Restoration and a new and permanent world-order (9:11-15). His words are often interpreted as a call for the Church to work for social justice on the grounds both that this is what God wants and that the blessings of a better world for all will follow.

However, this is to overlook the prophet's context. He ministered in about 760 BC, on the 'down' side of the graph charting Israel's experience of *salvation.* Although his pronouncements of *judgement* **include** the Gentile nations, he concentrates on the *Kingdom* of Israel (taking 'Israel' here to mean 'the Covenant people of God'—Amos actually prophesied particularly to the Southern Kingdom of Judah.) Though he calls for justice, Amos prophesies *judgement* based on a lack of Covenant-faithfulness on the part of the people. The social injustice of the nation stems not from their attitude to 'justice' but from their attitude to God: "You have not returned to *me*" (repeated five times in 4:6-11 !)

**Amos' call for Justice reflects not so much the potential for improvement as the inevitability of failure for a Godless society. God DEMANDS justice because this is right, but he inevitably WILL *judge* because people are evil.**

Is there, then, any *hope* in Amos? Certainly! First, the interceding prophet brings through his prayers some immediate relief from *judgement* (7:1-6), thus pointing to the need for Another who "always lives to intercede" for us (Hebrews 7:25). Secondly, the judgement will not be inescapable: "'Yet I will not totally destroy the house of Jacob,' says the LORD" (9:8), thus pointing to another avenue of escape from a greater judgement to come (Acts 2:40). Thirdly, it will be by the action of God IN FAITHFULNESS TO HIS *PROMISE* TO DAVID that what He seeks from people will come about: "'In that day **I will** restore David's fallen tent. **I will** repair its broken places, restore its ruins, and build it as it used to be ...' declares the LORD" (9:11), thus pointing to a greater act of God still to come.

Finally, the overall context of *salvation* history shows that this *fulfilment* did NOT take place at the Restoration of 538 BC—even though it was *hoped* for then. It therefore must refer to another *fulfilment* which lies in the future, which we now know is found in Jesus. However, this means that if we are to issue the call of Amos to our own society we must **first and foremost** call on the world to turn to God, to escape from the coming *judgement*, and to fix its *hopes* on Him for a renewal of creation.

**In the total context of *salvation-history*, to speak as Amos spoke is to PREACH THE GOSPEL.**

# *Fulfilment* and 'type'

You will begin to recognise by now that one of the keys to understanding the Bible is the idea of *fulfilment*. Sometimes there is a very graphic 'prefiguring' of *salvation* in the Old Testament fulfilled in the New by Jesus. This has been given the technical name of 'Typology', based on the Greek word for a "pattern" or "impression". For example, in Romans 5:14 we are told that Adam was literally "a **type** of the one to come", meaning Jesus. In

---

**ARE WE RIGHT ABOUT AMOS?**

Once again, people may question whether we are right about Amos. Are we not evading the Bible's call for social justice and slipping back into privatised Evangelical pietism? We would again answer firstly by stating that the interpretation works ENTIRELY WITHIN THE FRAMEWORK OF THE OLD TESTAMENT ITSELF. Secondly, again, we should see how the New Testament uses this passage. Here we have a clear confirmation, since the promise of Restoration in Amos 9 11-12 is used to refer to the BRINGING OF THE GOSPEL TO THE GENTILES (Acts 15:16-17). The New Testament writers are in no doubt that God is calling for a new world order. They also believe, however, that God Himself will bring this about in good time, and that our task is to make sure, **through evangelism now**, that people belong to that new world when it comes.

his time, Adam was like Jesus in that the fate of the human race rested on him and his decisions. Again in Hebrews 9:24 we are told, "Christ did not enter a man-made sanctuary that was only an **antitype** of the true one; he entered heaven itself." The man-made sanctuary of the Tent where God figuratively 'dwelt' (Exodus 25:8) represented the heavenly reality where God truly dwells.

Many other Old Testament people (Melchizedek, Joseph, David, etc.) and events (the Flood, the Exodus, the conquest of Canaan, etc.) may be seen as 'typological' pre-figurings of the *salvation* found in Jesus. Sometimes this is made explicit, sometimes not. However, we are not talking about ALLEGORIES, which would mean seeing Jesus represented in things which were originally nothing to do with him. Typology refers to situations where God graciously did through a **lesser and temporary medium** (such as "the blood of bulls and goats") what he would later do fully and permanently in Jesus.

This is the reason why we are not Jews! You may have wondered why the New Testament does not urge us to circumcise our males, avoid eating pork or keep the Friday-to-Saturday Sabbath. The answer is that given in Colossians 2:17, "**These are only a shadow of the things that were to come; the reality, however is found in Christ**."

What of the Old Testament food regulations, for example? These appear to be essential to God's Law, yet in Acts 10 we learn both of their significance and of their redundancy. Peter's vision where he is told to kill and eat unclean animals is accompanied by the voice of God saying "Do not call anything impure that God has made clean." He is then immediately directed by the Holy Spirit to evangelize a Gentile household without needing to require their circumcision. We thus discover what the food laws represented - the separation of God's holy people from unbelievers, **pre-figured in the Old Testament by food regulations which separated Jews from Gentiles**. In the New Testament the **principle** of separation remains, but the **substance** of that separation is now holy living: "Live such good lives among the pagans (i.e. the Gentiles) that ... they may see your good deeds and glorify God on the day he visits us." (1 Peter 2:12).

**Typological interpretation of the Bible, based on an understanding of the *salvation-historical* context,**

**prevents us from misapplying Old Testament events or practices in our own situation.**

# The life of the world to come—Amen!

We have seen that the Old Testament prophets from the time of Solomon onwards looked forward to a TOTAL TRANSFORMATION of creation in general and mankind in particular. We have also seen that this prophecy was *fulfilled* in Jesus. However, we must be careful to remember that the *fulfilment* of the *promise* in Jesus is itself NOT YET COMPLETED: "For he must reign until he has put all his enemies under his feet. The **last enemy** to be destroyed is death." (1 Corinthians 15:25-26). Death has not yet been destroyed (we still die!), therefore the *promise* is not yet totally *fulfilled*. The experience of *salvation* since the coming of Christ may itself be represented with a diagram:

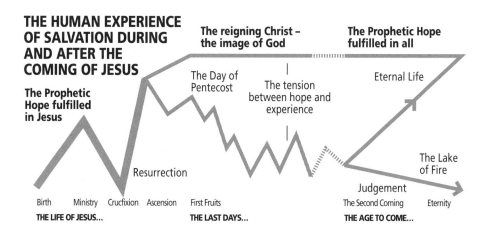

**THE HUMAN EXPERIENCE OF SALVATION DURING AND AFTER THE COMING OF JESUS**

The Prophetic Hope fulfilled in Jesus

The reigning Christ – the image of God

The Prophetic Hope fulfilled in all

The Day of Pentecost

The tension between hope and experience

Eternal Life

Resurrection

The Lake of Fire

Judgement

Birth · Ministry · Crucifixion · Ascension | First Fruits | The Second Coming · Eternity

**THE LIFE OF JESUS...** | **THE LAST DAYS...** | **THE AGE TO COME...**

The coming of Jesus into the world was the FIRST STAGE of the *fulfilment* of the *promise*. Jesus himself said, "**Today** this scripture (Isaiah 61:1-2) is *fulfilled* in your hearing" (Luke 4:21). However, the *hopes* which he raised in his followers seemed to be dashed by his crucifixion. As some of his disciples said before they knew of the resurrection, "The chief priests and our rulers handed him over to be sentenced to death, and they crucified him; but we had *hoped* that he was the one who was going to redeem Israel" (Luke 24:20-21). The realisation of His resurrection immediately caused these *hopes* to soar again: "Lord, are you *at this time* going to restore the *kingdom* to Israel?" (Acts 1:6). But the Ascension RE-INTRODUCED THE TENSION BETWEEN *HOPE* AND EXPERIENCE: "It is not for you to know the times or dates" (Acts 1:7).

The tension was to some extent resolved by the sending of the Holy Spirit at Pentecost. This formed the SECOND STAGE of the *fulfillment* of the *promise*, ushering in the "Last Days" foretold in the Old Testament: "These men are not drunk, as you suppose [...] No, this is what was spoken by the prophet Joel, 'In the last days, God says, I will pour out my Spirit on all people ...'" (Peter's speech, in Acts 2:16-17). In a crucial passage in Galatians 3:14 Paul actually IDENTIFIES the world-blessing *promised* to Abraham with the giving of the Spirit through Christ. (This suggests, contrary to traditional Charismatic teaching, that the Spirit is given ONCE to ALL Christians at conversion. We do not receive the *promise* and THEN the Spirit at a later date.)

However, the New Testament writers emphasise that the Spirit is received by us only as the FIRST FRUITS (Romans 8:23) of the *promise*, the GUARANTEE (2 Corinthians 1:22) of the Inheritance God has in store for his people. In Ephesians 1:13-14 Paul writes, "Having believed (in Christ), you were marked in him with a seal, the *promised* Holy Spirit, who is **a deposit guaranteeing our inheritance**." Here we see clearly the relationship of the Spirit to the *promise*. We have received the Spirit in *fulfilment* of the *promise* and the Spirit guarantees our Inheritance, but WE HAVE NOT YET RECEIVED THE INHERITANCE ITSELF. This will only happen in the THIRD STAGE of the *fulfilment* **when Christ returns**. This will also, however, be the point of God's final *judgement* on the wicked. At death or Christ's return, whichever comes sooner, our relationship with Him is fixed.

The inheritance which Christians are yet to receive is often referred to in the New Testament as our '*hope*'. The *hope* of the New Testament relates directly to the *hope* of the Old. However, the very fact that it is a *hope* once again emphasises the tension between this and our present experience: "We ourselves, who have the firstfruits of the Spirit, GROAN INWARDLY as we wait eagerly for our adoption as sons, the redemption of our bodies. For in this *hope* we were *saved*. But *hope* that is seen is no *hope* at all. Who *hopes* for what he already has?" (Romans 8:23-24). Until *hope* gives way to sight (or *fulfilment*) we DO NOT HAVE WHAT WE *HOPE* FOR—such as an immediate relationship with God, freedom from sickness or death, an end to temptation and sin, and so on.

In fact, our Christian experience is very similar to that of the people of the Old Testament who lived in the tension between their own *hope* and experience. An understanding that Jesus is the *fulfilment* of the *promise* is crucial to our interpretation of the Old Testament. In the same way, an understanding that the Holy Spirit has been given as THE FIRSTFRUITS BUT NOT THE FULLNESS of our *salvation* is crucial to our interpretation of the New:

> **We live in the period of tension between Jesus' First and Second Comings. Having the firstfruits of the Spirit, we live with both the *HOPE* OF GLORY and the EXPERIENCE OF SIN AND SUFFERING.**

We use the term **Eschatology** (pronounced 'es-kat-ology') to refer to the 'Last Things' concerned with the Second Coming of Jesus. '**Realised Eschatology**' refers to the foretaste of *salvation* we experience NOW—our new relationship with God, our sense of assurance, our new desire to pray and read the Bible, our mourning over sin and so on. However, a great danger for the Christian community has always been an '**Over-realised Eschatology**'—thinking that we have received everything now: "**Already** you have all you want! **Already** you have become rich! **You have become *kings***—and that without us!" (1 Corinthians 4:8). The desire to raise the dead through prayer, for example, may reflect a compassionate care for the bereaved or a desire to bring glory to God. Often, however, it springs from a wrong belief that we must have everything NOW in THIS WORLD.

# The Bible and the life of tension

How, then, should we regard our situation? The Christian perspective is established by the great '*Salvation* Act' of God revealed in the cross. However, we need to recognise that the human assessment of the cross and the Divine assessment are very different:

> **The Crucifixion, which appeared in human eyes to be a defeat, was in God's eyes the great point of VICTORY. It was the means by which sin was defeated, our forgiveness was obtained and by which we are RECONCILED WITH GOD. Thus it is the Crucifixion, rather than the Resurrection, which is the focus of the New Testament. PROPERLY SPEAKING, WE ARE A 'GOOD FRIDAY' PEOPLE EVEN MORE THAN WE ARE AN 'EASTER' PEOPLE!**

This was what Paul meant when he wrote, "Jews demand miraculous signs and Greeks look for wisdom, but we preach Christ crucified: a stumbling block to Jews and foolishness to Gentiles, but to those whom God has called, both Jews and Greeks, Christ the power of God and the wisdom of God." (1 Corinthians 1:22-24). When we trace the line of the human **experience** of *salvation* we must remember that the experience sometimes includes our IGNORANCE OF THE REALITIES: "How foolish you are, and how slow of heart to believe all that the prophets have spoken! Did not the Christ have to suffer these things?" (Luke 24:25). The 'message' of experience may sometimes appear to contradict the truth of God's love and power to care for us.

The Christian perspective must be governed by what the Bible reveals about God's plans, and not by our own ideas or experiences. This means we must look first to the PAST and the FUTURE rather than to our own PRESENT. 1 Peter 1:3-6 puts this clearly:

> "Praise be to the God and Father of our Lord Jesus Christ! In his great mercy he has given us new birth into a living *hope* through the RESURRECTION of Jesus Christ from the dead, and into an INHERITANCE that can never perish, spoil or fade—kept in HEAVEN for you, who through faith are shielded by God's power UNTIL the coming of the *salvation* that is ready to be revealed in the last time. In this you greatly rejoice, though NOW for a little while you may have had to suffer grief in all kinds of trials."

We see here that the Christian perspective consists of:

- **LOOKING BACK**—to Jesus, crucified and risen from the dead so that we can be born anew.
- **LOOKING UP**—to our Inheritance which is safe in heaven, as we are kept safe on earth by God's power.
- **LOOKING FORWARD**—to the Second Coming of Jesus when our *salvation* will be revealed.
- **LOOKING AROUND**—but only when we have looked back, up and forward because the situation we live in NOW is one of suffering "all kinds of trials". Peter says this is for "a little while"—but it will only seem like this when we see our sufferings in the context of *salvation* on the one hand and eternity on the other.

This also means that life lived now in the Spirit is not necessarily an endless round of miracles and direct experiences of God. Rather there is a tension between the way things are and the way we would like them to be—especially as regards our own behaviour (cf. Galatians 5:17). We still live in the time when we "*hope* for what we do not yet have" (Romans 8:25), so it will be perfectly normal for our experience sometimes to be encouraging, sometimes disappointing. The time when everything will be perfect still lies in the future.

# Reading the New Testament

The same perspective derived from Peter's letter helps us read the New Testament as it addresses the issues of the Christian life:

- **LOOKING BACK**—it points to Jesus, draws out the *fulfilment* of the Old Testament *promise* in Him (particularly his crucifixion) and gives us a proper understanding of the consequences.
- **LOOKING UP**—it emphasises our Heavenly citizenship and the call for Holy living, appropriate to those who now belong to the *Kingdom* of God.
- **LOOKING FORWARD**—it stresses the urgency of spreading the GOSPEL and believing in Jesus in the light of the coming *judgement*.

• **LOOKING AROUND**—it urges the Christian community to exercise PATIENCE AND PERSEVERANCE in the light of the coming *salvation*.

Read in this perspective, the New Testament is both our key to the Old Testament and our guide to the present life. We will not go into extremes of enthusiasm based on a desire for 'too much, too soon', nor will we be depressed by the disappointments of life based on wrong expectations. In short, we will not be "tossed back and forth by the waves, and blown here and there by every wind of teaching" (Ephesians 4:14).

## Conclusion to Part One

Hopefully, you now have a clearer idea of how the different parts of the Bible relate to one another. This should help you to a better understanding of each part as you read it. Rather than reading the Bible 'one dimensionally', ignoring the overall context of a book or passage, you will begin to develop a 'three dimensional' view of the Bible, seeing not only the words in the passage, but the passage in its setting within the Bible and within *salvation-history* as a whole. This should help you to read the Old Testament in a truly Christian manner and to understand your Christian experience in the present.

In Part Two we go on to look at practical approaches to Bible study—both good and bad.

# Methods of Bible study

# So you've read the Bible – what next?

A common consequence of someone becoming a Christian is that the Bible comes to life. A book that one day seemed big, boring and irrelevant is, the next day, full of interest and vitality. Suddenly, we cannot get enough of it, and we are soon surprised to find how much of it we've read.

**BRINGING THE WORD OF GOD TO LIFE IS A KEY WORK OF THE HOLY SPIRIT**. Paul writes in 1 Corinthians 2:12, "We have not received the spirit of the world, but the Spirit who is from God, THAT WE MAY UNDERSTAND what God has freely given us. This is what we speak, not in words taught us by human wisdom but in words taught by the Spirit, INTERPRETING SPIRITUAL TRUTHS TO SPIRITUAL MEN" (NIV footnote). **A true (but often neglected) sign of being 'spiritual' is a delight in the Bible.**

However, the day may come when we find we have finished reading the Bible—or at least the bits we can make sense of—and we start wondering what to do next. Most older Christians will have experienced the frustration of Bible study becoming dry. We may also have been in Bible Study groups which were, to say the least, unhelpful. If we're honest, many of them are boring! Bible study at this stage becomes like the contestants in the old radio panel game "Just a Minute"—consisting of **Repetition, Deviation or Hesitation:**

> **Repetition**—when we just repeat what the passage says in our own words: "These verses tells us we should 'love one another'. What are some examples of love? Whom do we mean by 'one another'?"—and so on *ad nauseam*.
> **Deviation**—when we deviate from the passage into our own ideas or, even worse, our own stories and anecdotes:

"That reminds me of ..."—and away we go!

**Hesitation**—when we are so bored by the previous two practices we hesitate to study the Bible at all!

These features are also common in many sermons, but REPETITION and DEVIATION in the pulpit are usually the result of HESITATION in the study !

# The underlying problem

Part of the difficulty when we get to this stage is that WE DON'T KNOW WHAT THE PROBLEM IS—so our solutions are usually wrong! We realise the Bible hasn't changed. We are still keen to study it—which is why we perhaps try to go to a group every week, or open it every day. But we just don't seem to be getting anywhere. Remembering how interesting the Bible seemed when they first became Christians, and how often they read it then, many people assume their problem is either LOSS OF FIRST LOVE or LACK OF DISCIPLINE. This suggests the following solutions (and usually leads to disappointing results):

**Loss of First Love**—if the Bible hasn't changed, it must be me! If it was the Holy Spirit who first made the Bible interesting, maybe a LACK of the Holy Spirit is making the Bible dull now.

The solution is MORE OF THE HOLY SPIRIT. But the result is usually that I now have two problems: I still can't get more out of the Bible, and I don't have more of the Spirit either.

**Lack of Discipline**—if I could only be more REGULAR in Bible study perhaps it would become interesting again.

The solution is to BUY SOME BIBLE STUDY NOTES. The result is usually that after six weeks I can now see at a glance how much further I've fallen behind in my Bible study.

Now there may be some truth in either of these analyses. If something really is wrong with my life spiritually then Bible study may be affected. Equally, Bible study does require discipline—it doesn't just 'happen'. However, the very fact that **most Christians at some point run out of steam in studying the**

**Bible** should suggest to us that it is a stage of spiritual development which is common to all and that therefore it may be a symptom of growth rather than a sign of trouble.

> **Reaching the point where OLD FORMS of Bible study fail to satisfy indicates that IT IS TIME TO MOVE ON TO *NEW FORMS* of Bible study.**

## Leaving what lies behind

Part of the process of growing as a Christian is realising that there are certain forms of Bible study that we need to leave behind. Some are simply the early practices of our spiritual infancy (cf. 1 Corinthians 3:1-2). They are nothing to be ashamed of, we are just too old for them. Others, however, are forms we may have learned later in our Christian lives but which are WRONG and which we need to UNLEARN if we are to grow.

**Read it and Close it:** In our spiritual infancy Bible passages often strike us with great force and clarity on a first read-through. Particular verses may well 'leap out' with all the force of a personal message from God—even though this may sometimes be regardless of the context (or even the content) of the passage. Most of us start here, and there is nothing wrong with it, especially if the stories and ideas in the Bible are unfamiliar.

**Devotional Bible Study:** This is becoming increasingly popular in evangelical circles but is actually a reversion to a pre-Reformation practise called '*lectio divina*' ('holy reading'). The key question we ask is, "What does this passage make me FEEL about God, or myself or the world around me?" We may even be encouraged to heighten the feelings by specific techniques: repeating verses over and over, or imagining ourselves to be a character (or even an object!) in a narrative. The measure of the effectiveness of this form of study will always be HOW I FELT at the end of it rather than how well I understood the passage.

**I-Ching for Christians:** The Chinese book of the *I-Ching* is a collection of writings which are used as guidance in various situations. The user divines which section to turn to and adapts the advice given there to his context. Many Christians treat the Bible the same way, either trusting verses found at random or turning over pages to find a passage that 'speaks to' them. THIS IS PROBABLY THE WORST FORM OF BIBLE STUDY and doesn't really deserve the name at all.

**Spiritual Brownie Points:** (also known as the 'Read and Right' method). Here we 'Read' the Bible to stay on the 'Right' side of God. Underlying this is often the belief that the day will somehow 'go better' if I have read the Bible at the start. Since it plays on guilt, it is also an approach encouraged by some cults. However, it is not really Bible Study at all since the aim is not to understand the Bible but to perform the 'good work' of reading. It may turn out to be the last stage before giving up reading the Bible altogether.

All these methods of Bible study are things we need to leave behind—and in the case of the last two are things we would be well advised not to start doing in the first place.

# A 'sophisticated' approach to the Bible

Our goal is to study the Bible more effectively. To know what is effective, however, we need to be clear about the precise nature of our goal, so that we can see whether our studies are getting us there. Fortunately, the Bible tells us what effective Bible study aims at:

> **"...from infancy you have known the Holy Scriptures, which are able to make you wise for salvation through faith in Jesus Christ. All Scripture is God-breathed and is useful for teaching, rebuking, correcting and training in righteousness, so that the man of God may be thoroughly equipped for every good work."** *(2 Timothy 3:15-17)*

**EFFECTIVE BIBLE STUDY KEEPS US IN THE WAY OF SALVATION AND EQUIPS US TO DO GOOD WORKS.**

This passage points to an alternative approach to Bible study:

**The "Sophisticated" Approach:** Paul tells Timothy that the Scriptures are able to make him "WISE for salvation". The word for "wise" is literally 'sophisai', from which we get 'sophisticated'. Our reading of the Bible should be just that – aiming at wisdom! **Inspiration BY the Bible should come from understanding OF the Bible**.

## We ask the questions

The key to understanding the Bible is ASKING THE RIGHT QUESTIONS OF THE PASSAGE. The knack is knowing just which questions to ask! Jesus' example in Mark 12:35-37 is a practical demonstration of this:

> "While Jesus was teaching in the temple courts, he asked, 'How is it that the teachers of the law say that the Christ is the son of David? David himself, speaking by the Holy Spirit, declared: "The Lord said to my Lord: 'Sit at my right hand until I put your enemies under your feet.'" David himself calls him "Lord". HOW THEN CAN HE BE HIS SON?'"

The traditional interpretation of the passage was right as far as it went—the Messiah would indeed be the Son of David, and many Old Testament passages testified to this. However, BY ASKING THE RIGHT QUESTION -"How can David's 'Lord' be his son?"—Jesus showed that the traditional interpretation didn't go far enough! We need to learn this knack of asking questions to get at the heart of a passage.

There are three questions which it is always useful to ask:

**1. What is the passage saying?**
**2. Why is it saying it?**
**3. Why is it saying it here?**

### 1. WHAT IS THE PASSAGE SAYING?
**The first priority is to read what the passage ACTUALLY says, not what we THINK it says.**

Too often we think we know what a passage is saying and therefore we don't read what is written. The teachers of the Law whom Jesus criticised thought they knew what David must be saying, so they missed part of what he had written. As a result, they didn't understand the passage.

Look back at the passage we quoted from 2 Timothy 3:15-17. Is Paul merely telling Timothy the Bible is a good thing? Ask yourself, "Is there anything here I don't understand—any words or concepts? Is there anything I've never noticed before?" It may be useful to read the passage in more than one translation to help you look at it more closely.

## 2. WHY IS IT SAYING IT?

But we need to go beyond mere comprehension. Here are some other questions we might ask:

> • *WHY does Paul say, "WISE for salvation"? What has wisdom to do with being saved?*
> • *WHY does he talk about "good work", and why does he refer to "EVERY good work"?*

We should also be asking supplementary questions:

> • *If salvation is connected with wisdom, how important is our understanding of doctrine?*
> • *How does Scripture make us wise? What does it make us wise about?*
> • *How does Scripture equip us for good works?*
> • *If Scripture equips us for **every** good work, do we need extra guidance from outside the Bible?*
> • *If the Bible doesn't give guidance about a particular activity— e.g. smoking—can we say whether it is good or not?*

Some people may also have even more complex questions, though these are not so essential:

> • *What does Paul mean by Scripture?*
> • *What does the phrase "God-breathed" mean in v.16?*
> • *Should we count 2 Timothy as Scripture and why? (2 Peter 3:16 helps on this one!)*

There are no hard and fast rules about which questions to ask, and asking the right ones is partly intuitive—a bit like being a detective—but the more you practise doing it, the better you will become.

### 3. WHY IS IT SAYING IT HERE?

We shouldn't, however, stop our questioning at this point. We need also to ask, "WHY IS THE PASSAGE SAYING WHAT IT IS SAYING *HERE*?" Why, for example, does Paul write in such basic terms to Timothy, of all people? You would have thought Timothy would hardly need telling! Could it be that the Apostle's assistant is in danger of underestimating the importance of Scripture? (Compare this passage with I Timothy 4:13-16.) If this is so, perhaps we—even those of us who are church elders—might face the same danger and need the same warning.

When we ask "Why is the passage saying what it is saying *here?*", the concept of "here" includes more than the immediate paragraph, chapter or book. There is also the audience to whom the book was originally addressed. Sometimes we can work out who they were from the book itself - 1 and 2 Thessalonians, for example, are clearly written to the Christians at Thessalonica. Sometimes, however, we will need to go to the commentaries or a Bible dictionary for guidance. An awareness of the audience is often vital to a proper understanding of the Bible. To whom, for example, is the "Sermon on the Mount" addressed? If we see it as a proclamation addressed to 'all and sundry' we will interpret it differently compared with seeing it **as it really is**—addressed to the disciples of Jesus.

The context of a passage also includes the setting of the book in which it is found within its **theological**, **historical** and **cultural** framework. In the case of 2 Timothy, for example, we need to see that this is an exhortation from Paul who is expecting to die at any time (4:6-8)—though he is uncertain as to when that time will be (4:9-13). He is preparing Timothy for life and ministry in the future when the foundations of the Gospel have been laid, but the threat of false teaching is everywhere. This explains why it concentrates not so much on the basics of the faith as on the responsibilities of the church elder, especially in teaching. At the same time, because it looks forward to the period after the age of the Apostles—the age we are now living in—it is of great relevance to us in issues of authority and Christian conduct.

We need to cultivate this habit of always reading a verse within a passage, a passage within a chapter, a chapter within a book, a book within the Bible and finally everything in its historical and cultural context.

**In particular, we must learn to read each book in its *'salvation-historical'* context as outlined in Part One. WE MUST IDENTIFY THE HUMAN EXPERIENCE OF *SALVATION* ASSOCIATED WITH THE BOOK IF WE ARE TO APPLY ITS LESSONS PROPERLY TO OURSELVES TODAY.**

On the other hand WE MUST STOP TREATING THE BIBLE AS A SERIES OF 'VERSES' DETACHED FROM A CONTEXT. Although the practice of dividing the Bible into chapters and verses is useful as an aid to finding our way around, it can be quite destructive when it comes to studying what the Bible says. We need to understand that the Bible did not descend from Heaven as a series of 'Christmas Cracker' style mottoes. It is a book of whole books and needs to be read as such.

## Beginning, middle and end

There is an old complaint about books or plays which have a beginning, a middle and an end, "but not necessarily in that order". These are usually works where the author has tried too hard to be clever. However, there is a serious point here—we expect a book to have a STRUCTURE which helps us makes sense of it.

Due to our bad habits, however, WE DON'T USUALLY LOOK FOR THIS IN THE BIBLE. We break the Bible up into fragments— 'verses' or 'readings' which give a very false impression. Yet ALMOST EVERY BOOK IN THE BIBLE WAS WRITTEN TO BE READ AS ONE PIECE. The Epistles or Revelation, for example, would have been read straight through to the congregations for whom they were written. The Gospels similarly tell a complete story from beginning to end—and may indeed have been written as evangelistic tracts. Only a few books like Psalms or Proverbs seem designed for reading in 'bits'. IT IS THEREFORE ESSENTIAL TO GET INTO THE HABIT OF READING WHOLE BOOKS. We should not regard reading a whole Gospel straight through as a 'superhuman achievement'! Of course, to get the most out of a book we will want to spend some time studying its details. But the details only make full sense in the context of the whole.

To begin with, we may be aware of only the most simple aspects of structure. Isaiah, for example, divides basically into two:

**Part 1. Chapters 1-39**: THREAT—the prophet concentrates on the consequences of sin and judgement.
**Part 2. Chapters 40-66**: PROMISE—the prophet looks forward to God's action of redeeming both His people and all Creation.

Even as simple a division as this, however, helps us get our bearings. Eventually we will want to make our analysis more detailed. As we do so, we will often find there is a more complex pattern to a book. Thus Daniel follows a carefully crafted outline:

| | |
|---|---|
| **Chapter 1** | Biographical introduction |
| **Chapter 2 (A)** | **DREAM**—Nebuchadnezzar's dream of the Future |
| **Chapter 3 (B)** | **DELIVERANCE**—from the Fiery Furnace |
| **Chapter 4 (C)** | **MERCY**—on King Nebuchadnezzar |
| **Chapter 5 (C')** | **JUDGEMENT**—on King Belshazzar |
| **Chapter 6 (B')** | **DELIVERANCE**—from the Den of Lions |
| **Chapter 7 (A')** | **DREAM**—Daniel's dream of the Future |
| **Chapters 8-12** | Daniel's Visions of the Future |

This analysis is very helpful to us in revealing the relationship of the themes in chapters 2-7. They follow a pattern known technically as a 'chiasm', from the Greek letter chi (X—pronounced 'ki' as in 'kite'), meaning a 'crossing over'—ABC X C'B'A'. This is a very common pattern in the Bible. Recognising it here means that we should compare chapter 2 with chapter 7, 3 with 6 and 4 with 5. When we do this we will get more from them than we would by reading them on their own as we see their differences and similarities.

Most Bible commentaries will give you this sort of structural analysis. However, it is good to get into the habit of working it out yourself with a pen and paper as you read through a book. This will not only make you more aware of the structure but will also make you look at the Bible more carefully. (Bear in mind that the actual structure doesn't always follow the chapter divisions— these were added much later.) Of course, you may well find that your analysis disagrees with that of the commentaries. **There is no harm in this**—structures are to a certain extent a matter for debate. You may be right and they may be wrong! In any case, it is good to have our ideas criticised in this way. Humility is one of the steps towards becoming a better Bible student.

However, we must remember that identifying the structure is not an end in itself. Too many books and commentaries stop with an outline of the structure of a book which is little better than a 'Contents' page. We must go on to consider how the structure reveals the theme or 'plot' of a book—the flow of thought in the author's mind and the point at which he is aiming. DESCRIBING the structure helps us see the wood from the trees. ANALYSING the structure allows us to see not merely the shape of the 'wood' but the significance of the 'trees' within it.

> **Analysing the structure of a Bible book will help us:**
> **1. Understand the links between the various parts.**
> **2. Detect the author's themes and purposes.**
> **3. Be aware of the similarities and contrasts between different parts of the book.**
> **4. Highlight the lessons of the part we are studying.**

# Putting it all together

We can now begin to put all our lessons together and it is perhaps best to do this by looking at a sample passage such as Mark 8:14-15:

> "The disciples had forgotten to bring bread, except for one loaf they had with them in the boat. 'Be careful,' Jesus warned them. 'Watch out for the yeast of the Pharisees and that of Herod.'"

This is a very familiar passage which most people understand to be a warning against hypocrisy—and this is partly born out by Jesus' words in Luke 12:1, "Be on your guard against the yeast of the Pharisees, which is hypocrisy." But Mark has a deeper lesson to teach us about the **nature** of the Pharisees' behaviour and its **dangers** for all of us which go beyond mere 'play acting'. This becomes clearer when we look at the passage in its context and ask the right questions of it. The first step is to look at the structure of the passage.

## 1. THE BOOK IN THE BIBLE

Mark is, of course, a Gospel, but we need to remember the '*salvation*-historical' context of the Gospels. In them the *promises* of God about the coming *Kingdom* are *fulfilled* in the person of Jesus. NOTICE HOW THE PURPOSE OF MARK 1:1-8 IS TO SET THE BOOK IN ITS BIBLICAL AND '*SALVATION*-HISTORICAL' CONTEXT. We also see that Jesus the *King* is rejected by his people. Mark 8:14-15 is part of this total story.

## 2. THE PASSAGE IN THE BOOK

Where, then, does the present passage fit in the structure of Mark's Gospel? We can divide the Gospel roughly into two:

> **Part 1. (1:1-10:45) BEFORE JERUSALEM**—Jesus, the promised King, preaches the Kingdom and teaches the disciples.
> **Part 2. (10:46-16:8\*) IN JERUSALEM**—Jesus, the rejected King, is crucified and rises from the dead. (*The best manuscripts of Mark do not contain vv.9-20 of chapter 16, and they probably do not form part of his original ending.)

Part 1 can then be divided into two again:

> **Part 1. BEFORE JERUSALEM**
> **A. (1:1-8:26) The Messiah hidden**—Prior to Peter's confession (8:29) Jesus reveals himself as the Messiah to the 'eye of faith' by word and action.
> **B. (8:27-10:45) The Messiah revealed**—Following Peter's confession that he is the Messiah, Jesus teaches about his true nature and his coming death and resurrection.

Our passage belongs to the end of **Part 1 A**, where Jesus has not

declared himself openly to Israel but where the disciples have seen
and heard enough to suggest to them his identity as Messiah. We
would therefore expect the passage to have something to do with
the question of WHO JESUS IS.

## 3. THE VERSES IN THE PASSAGE

We can now set these verses in their immediate context in the
surrounding passage:

| | |
|---|---|
| 13 | Leaving the unbelieving Pharisees. |
| **14-15** | **Jesus' warning**. |
| 16 | The disciples' misunderstanding. |
| 17-18 | Jesus' question comparing the disciples with the unbelieving crowds (cf. 4 :11-12). |
| 19-20 | The lesson of the feeding miracles. |
| 21 | The incomprehension of the disciples and a final question from Jesus. |

Having looked at the structure and set the verses in their
context, it is time to ask our standard questions.

## 4. WHAT IS HE SAYING?

We should bear in mind that "he" actually refers to **two** speakers
here! One is Jesus, and it is his words we will concentrate on first.
However, the other is **Mark** who is recounting his Gospel in a
particular way to teach us, the readers, a particular lesson. We
will look at Mark's contribution more in the section on "Why is he
saying it here?"

The question "What is he saying?" is firstly one of
comprehension. Do we understand the meaning of the key
phrases and words in the passage?

**Be careful**—the overall theme of the passage.
**Yeast**—the key illustration used in the passage.
**Pharisees**—the villains of the passage.
**Herod**—another villain.

## 5. WHY IS HE SAYING IT?

We have identified four crucial 'concepts' in these verses, the
warning, yeast, Pharisees and Herod. Why are they mentioned?

**The warning**—both Jesus and Mark are sounding a warning. There is a danger both to the disciples and to Mark's readers!

**Yeast**—actually, the word "leaven" would be more accurate. "Yeast" for us is something hygienic we buy from the supermarket in packets. In Jesus' day, leaven was a fermented lump of old dough carried over into a new batch of bread to make it rise. It was also the substance which was expunged from Jewish houses at the Passover (Exodus 12:15) and stood for the corruptions of the old life which could threaten the new (cf. 1 Corinthians 5:8; Galatians 5:9)! There is a fundamental issue of salvation at stake here.

**Pharisees**—their negative example is detailed in the preceding verses (8:11-12). After all that Jesus has done (e.g. 2:1-12), they are STILL testing him and asking for proof.

**Herod**—a whole section is devoted to Herod in 6:14-29. Herod is a regular listener to the imprisoned John the Baptist (6:20) but is unable ever to respond to his preaching. In the end, he has John killed.

What, then, is the 'leaven' of the Pharisees and Herod? It seems to be A CONTINUAL FAILURE TO RESPOND TO THE GOSPEL IN SPITE OF REPEATEDLY SEEING AND HEARING THINGS WHICH CALL FOR REPENTANCE AND FAITH.

### 6. WHY IS HE SAYING IT HERE?

Just as there are two speakers here, Jesus and Mark, so there are two audiences—the disciples to whom Jesus is talking, and the Gospel reader for whom Mark is writing. We will look at the significance of the words of each speaker to each audience in turn.

**Jesus speaks here as he does because the disciples are in danger of behaving like the Pharisees and Herod. Though they are constantly in Jesus' presence, hearing and seeing his words and deeds, they have not yet responded in faith.**

Mark, however, also wants his audience to question themselves. How are they responding? Have they begun to see who Jesus is, and to turn to him in repentance and faith, or are

they, like the Pharisees and Herod, going to ask for another
sermon, another miracle?

**Mark speaks as he does here because the reader is
also in danger—of having read this far in the Gospel
and yet failed to respond to Jesus.**

Mark writes to produce an effect in the reader. In a similar way,
each of the four Gospels is a theological work rather than a mere
biography. It is useful for us to think of the Gospels, in common
with the rest of the Bible, as God's teaching material aimed at us.
This passage provides excellent (and carefully structured)
material for a sermon for 'fringe' people who can never make up
their minds about Jesus.

**The more effectively we analyse a Bible passage, the
more readily the message it actually contains reveals
itself and the less we have to struggle to 'find' a
message hidden within it.**

Having gained a basic understanding of the passage, we may
now go on to ask other questions and look in more detail at its
application to our lives—but we will now do so in a proper and
effective way, not based on our feelings about the passage, much
less on our feelings about ourselves, but on the lessons intended
by Jesus and Mark.

# Taught not caught

We are almost at the end of this booklet. However, I want to
conclude with some remarks about the importance of Bible
teaching. There is a popular saying that Christianity is "caught,
not taught" but it is, unfortunately, nonsense and dangerous
nonsense at that. A quick glance through the Bible will show that
although many religious ideas may be "caught" Christianity is
not one of them. The Great Commission says as much: "Go and
make disciples (students) of all nations, baptising them in the
name of the Father and of the Son and of the Holy Spirit, and
TEACHING them to observe everything I have commanded you."
In Acts 28:31, we are told that in Rome Paul "Boldly and without

hindrance ... preached the Kingdom of God and TAUGHT about the Lord Jesus Christ." The Apostles in Acts 4:18 are forbidden to "speak or TEACH at all in the name of Jesus". But in the very next chapter we find they are back before the court being told, "We gave you strict orders not to TEACH in this name ... Yet you have filled Jerusalem with your TEACHING" (5:28). No-one objects to them quietly living the Christian life in the hope that it might rub off on their neighbours, but TEACHING THE GOSPEL creates enemies!

Teaching is also linked to spiritual growth as well as conversion. In Ephesians 4 we are told that Christ gave the Church four great ministries of the word—apostles, prophets, evangelists and pastor-teachers "to prepare God's people for works of service, so that the body of Christ may be built up" (4:11-12). When this process is complete, "we will no longer be infants, tossed back and forth by the waves, and blown here and there by every wind of TEACHING" (4:14).

Moreover, it is in the area of teaching that Satan most likes to attack the church: "The Spirit clearly says that in later times some will abandon the faith and follow deceiving spirits and things TAUGHT by demons. Such TEACHINGS come through hypocritical liars..." (Tim. 4:1-2). The best antidote to **deceitful** teaching is **sound** teaching. Timothy is told in the same letter, "Watch your life and your **doctrine** (teaching) closely. Persevere in them, because IF YOU DO, YOU WILL SAVE BOTH YOURSELF AND YOUR HEARERS." However, one of the tragedies of today is that teaching is given second place in church to what is often mere entertainment. As Paul warned in 2 Timothy 4:3, "The time will come [and, we may perhaps say, 'now is'] when men will not put up with sound doctrine. Instead, to suit their own desires, they will gather around them a great number of teachers to say what their itching ears want to hear." FAR TOO MANY CHRISTIAN ACTIVITIES, SERMONS AND BOOKS SIMPLY SCRATCH WHERE PEOPLE ITCH. We need to allow Scripture to scratch us where we DON'T itch.

There are many passages in Scripture to show us that the rôle of church elders is to teach people Scripture itself:

**Luke 24:45-47**, "Then he opened their minds so they could UNDERSTAND THE SCRIPTURES. He told them, 'This is WHAT IS WRITTEN: The Christ will suffer and rise from the dead on the third day, and repentance and forgiveness of sins will be preached in his name to all nations, beginning at Jerusalem.'"

**John 20:30-31**, "Jesus did many other miraculous signs in the presence of his disciples, which are not recorded in this book. But THESE ARE WRITTEN that you may believe that Jesus is the Christ, the Son of God, and that by believing you may have life in his name."

**Romans 16:25-26**, "Now to him who is able to establish you by my gospel and the proclamation of Jesus Christ, according to the revelation of the mystery hidden for long ages past, but now revealed and made known through the PROPHETIC WRITINGS by the command of the eternal God, so that all nations might believe and obey him..."

**Revelation 1:3**, "Blessed is the one who READS THE WORDS of this prophecy, and blessed are those who hear and take to heart WHAT IS WRITTEN in it."

However, even if you are not yourself a church elder, the message is clear -we are to endeavour to UNDERSTAND the Scriptures as best we can. This means that our focus in Bible study should be on STUDY—not quantity, intensity or emotion. We are mistaken to believe that the way to the soul is through the heart. The proper and Biblical way to the soul is THROUGH THE MIND—that is to say, through our thoughts rather than through our feelings. In the Bible, the "hard heart" is not a lack of emotion but an unbelieving attitude. (Psalm 119 gives the right relationship between 'heart' and 'head'.) Naturally the heart will also be touched when the mind is reached—but it will be touched in the right way and for the right reasons.

**Our being built up by the Bible depends on our grasping the MEANING of the passage first and foremost.**

# Accurate teaching *vs* effective learning

Finally, we need to emphasise one other reason why we are studying the Bible, in order to make sure that our studies contribute to this goal. As in the rest of our Christian life, our aim is to become more like Jesus—to be "conformed to the likeness of God's Son".

It is an excellent thing if a church elder or Bible Study group leader aims to teach the Bible accurately. However, THIS IS NOT AN END IN ITSELF. It is of no use to teach the Bible accurately if it doesn't result in changed lives. As James says, "Anyone who listens to the word but does not do what it says is like a man who looks at his face in a mirror and, after looking at himself, goes away and immediately forgets what he looks like." (1:23-24). Jesus puts it more bluntly: "Why do you call me 'Lord, Lord' and do not do what I say?" (Luke 6:46).

It is unfortunately true that Bible study can sometimes be a substitute for other, personally more costly, forms of Christian behaviour. Churches where the Bible is revered in theory are not always places where lives are transformed in practise. What does your church make of Matthew 6:19-21, 1 Corinthians 7:27, Ephesians 4:15 or James 2:3-4, for example? The Bible should constantly be making us feel uncomfortable, stimulating us to change our behaviour so as to bring it in line with the Gospel.

TEACHING IS USELESS IF IT IS NOT ACCOMPANIED BY LEARNING. I may be the world's finest Bible teacher, but if I am speaking in English and my audience only understands Swahili then I am wasting my time. Similarly, if I am speaking to unbelievers or lazy Christians, my words will fall on deaf ears unless the Spirit of God is at work to bring about change—see Acts 13:48 for a dramatic example of this! LEARNING is what counts, but learning can only be measured by CHANGE. This is not to say that we should be constantly trying to squeeze a 'practical application' out of our Bible studies. The application should, and generally will, follow naturally from a right understanding of the text. However, we have to make absolutely sure that we do not stifle practical application because it is too uncomfortable for us. The hard heart and the deaf ear go together in Scripture. Each time we come to the Bible our prayer should echo that of the Psalmist:

**"Search me, O God, and know my heart; test me and know my anxious thoughts. See if there is any offensive way in me, and lead me in the way everlasting."**

NOTES

NOTES